Forex Trading Tips

The Complete Guide To Successful Forex Trading

Introduction

Have you ever asked yourself: Why to select forex trading? Well, here are some steps on how to perform forex trading investment.

How to Get Started:

To get the things started, you need a computer, the internet connection, software, broker, initial investment, and strategy. To learn more, you can take the help of the starter kit.

Trading Fee:

To start the trade on an immediate basis, you need capital as low as $25. When you earn a lot of profits, you can do it again and again.

Proper trading:

Another reason to do forex trading forex trading is you can even work from anywhere at any time depending upon your comfort and convenience.

You can work at your pace and enhance the confidence. Some of the platforms require you to learn tricks of the trade and by using a dummy account, you can learn the same. The forex trading is considered as self-paced trading. It just means that you don't need any special assistance in this trading.

You don't need to sit and do the duty for eight hours. It is way beyond the conventional job, and you need to do trading for two hours per week. Thus, making it less than 40 hours and adding to your convenience.

Profits:

To earn a huge amount of profits, you need to maintain a good relationship with the broker. It is too simple to trade and even to make profits.

The use of forex trading platform is required to pay you 10% of the transaction cost. It is the primary reason that brokers don't charge any commission, as they have already obtained spread.

Manpower:

The forex trading doesn't require any stress of performance evaluation, payroll, job interviews and the like.

You need to deal simply with the brokers, not with the employees. If you need a new agent, there are many of them waiting down the line. When you trade with a broker, all you need is a sufficient margin.

There is no requirement for vendors, customers, liquidation or anything else.

Equipment:

To become a forex trader all you need is a simple computer and no major equipment is required. No need for daily inventory

Unlike conventional professions, there is no need for a formal degree.

Proper education and strategy is the best way to succeed in the field of the forex market.

Self- Education:

Another reason why to join forex trading is the resources are made available to you so that you can learn about the things yourself. If you bet start using the minimum amount that is required to trade, they have one to one tutorial that is great.

You can learn the basics of forex trading with a small margin. With proper training and experience, you can crack on how to succeed in this market.

Thanks for downloading this book. It's my firm belief that it will provide you with all the answers to your questions

Chapter 1: How to Get Started

Have you ever thought of making cash in the privacy of your home? Work as much or as little as you like. Forex trading, or the trading of foreign currencies, allows you to do just that-- make money at home.

The foreign currency trading market is the least regulated market in the world. Nevertheless, it's also the world's largest financial market.

From the outside, trading in the forex market may appear to be done without difficulty. Nevertheless, that's not the case, at all. For beginning traders, proper education and training in the basics are of paramount significance. Trading the way the professionals do it is certainly possible. It's just like any other occupation: It requires knowledge and experience.

Training in this discipline is readily available. You can find formal classroom training. However, online training is also accessible, and it's the kind that many people want these days. Online training allows personal study from home. Regardless of which method is used, the student will benefit from the training when he or she starts making successful trades. Moreover, it's possible to offset the initial cost of the program.

The courses for those who would like to become professional traders offer education in all of the aspects of trading. You'll have access to the latest software and tools required for successful forex trading. The professionals use the best tools available to them, and through their teaching, they'll be able to help you select the best tools for your trading.

For forex trading, a significant amount of knowledge is required. Not anyone with any business acumen at all would embark upon a new field without the correct training. Financial disaster awaits those who are less than astute. To do well as a trader in the forex market, a fundamental knowledge of foreign currency exchange is demanded.

Training courses, online or off, offer the student the advantage of using real date and quotes. Also, the student learns skills that would take years to accomplish otherwise. How to write a business plan is part of the education process, and when combined with the instructor's feedback, provides a good foundation for writing the next scheme.

Successful forex trading means that the trader can make a lot of money in a short amount of time. To be successful, however, requires training, experience, and patience.

If you are a forex trader, you have probably heard a whole lot of different trading advice, trading rules, etc. In certainty, there are several general rules when it comes down to trading forex. Unfortunately, most traders, especially the newbie traders who are just starting out in the forex market, will break these rules. Part of the process of education is breaking rules and making mistakes. In doing so, a trader will ultimately form their personal trading skills, and they'll develop their set of trading rules and laws. They, in the long run, will bring you to success.

Before you can even start thinking about developing your personal set of forex trading rules and guidelines, you have to evaluate your knowledge of the industry thoroughly. Some people prematurely feel that they have acquired all of the necessary knowledge they will ever need to become successful forex traders. Unfortunately, more often than not, this is not the case.

It always seems to come back to proper and thorough forex training. The best forex training involves educating yourself or hiring someone else to educate you on each and every aspect of everything trading forex entails. Luckily, there are recommended factors that can help you on your journey to becoming a successful forex trader.

Here are some general recommendations to help you avoid significant losses in your first stages of trading forex:

When you are first starting out, decide on the specific amount of money you want to use to begin your initial forex trading with. This sum of money must be an amount you are willing to risk losing.

When trading, you should never use any more than 10% of your initial deposit. Never used borrowed or loaned money for trading forex, always use your means.

Never make too many transactions at the same time. Doing so will increase your possibilities of making mistakes.

Never work against the general trend. Always analyze at least two sources of information (i.e. news and graphic analysis) Also, always be sure to evaluate the situation before you enter the market. Never change your opinion based on forecasts of other people when your position is already open.

Never practice "emotional" trading, and always rest of at least 24 hours after you either make a large profit or suffer a large loss.

Continue to practice, maintain, and even improve your level of discipline. Also, keep on improving your normal, stable professional estimation of your possibilities.

If you don't know when you have to close a transaction with losses or when you have to fix the profit, do not make the transaction.

Be sure to install the stop loss to cut your losses. Also, install the take profit to fix profits. Your take profit should be at least twice as large as your stop loss.

Do not use the "lock" method if you do not understand what it is.

Those are just some general recommendations for those who may just be starting out in the forex market

Chapter 2: Forex Trading Plan

Many people have turned to forex trading in the last couple of years in the hope of earning some extra money, and possibly with the hope of getting seriously rich as well. However, it is tough to make money from forex trading which is why you should always approach it with a solid trading plan in place.

If you are going to make long-term profits, then you need to take it seriously, which means having a well-thought-out plan of attack. This all starts with the trading system you plan on using.

Before you even think about trading with real money, you need to do lots and lots of testing and experiment with various technical indicators to find a system that's going to make your money on a consistent basis. It doesn't have to be perfect, and indeed a perfect system doesn't even exist, but it should have the ability to grow your account in the long run.

It may only have a success rate of 40-50%, but this can be more than enough to generate some decent profits. For instance, if you use a stop loss of 20 points and target 60 points per trade, then a win ratio of 40-50% would generate some very healthy returns.

Some other key components of a forex trading plan include discipline and money management. Let's start with discipline first of all because if you're going to become a profitable trader, then you need to create a productive system and you need to have the discipline to stick to this system. Winning traders accept that losing trades are a part of the game, but the traders who end up losing money are those that have difficulty accepting losses and subsequently start chasing losses, just like a lot of gamblers do.

Money management is important too because even if you have a profitable system, you should still only risk a small percentage of your capital on any one trade. Your goal should be to grow your account steadily over time and by only risking say 2 or 3% per trade you can build your account very nicely as your capital starts to grow.

So to sum up, if you're serious about becoming a successful forex trader you should create, and stick to a solid trading plan. This should incorporate a profitable trading system, a disciplined approach to trading, and sound money management principles.

Chapter 3: Forex Trading Strategies

A currency market is a great place for investors to put their money to make good profits. This market is free of any external control and can be worked around the clock. Currency trading systems are trading platforms that can be much automated. A currency-trading platform is the best tool you can use to develop your effective forex trading strategy that will maximize turnover.

A trading system can help individuals who are new to trading and can assist those who have been trading a long time. Trading software can be bought from the internet, and you can install it on your computer. All you need is a high-speed internet connection to run these programs.

Many companies offer you virtual training programs. In case you are a newcomer and don't want to lose money to start, you can use the virtual training programs or demo accounts. In these programs, you virtually trade in currencies while in receipt of practice. This training provides a practical experience.

After this, you can move ahead with the real-time trading. Thus, my first advice to you is to open a demo account and understand the fundamentals involved in forex trading. Forex trading also offers the opening a mini account where you can begin by investing as little as $50 or $100. With such little money at stake, you can apply all your knowledge and see how it works. Once you are confident, you can open a regular account and start currency trading with larger numbers.

On the internet, there are many forex service providers. You must conduct proper research about the providers and the systems that they offer. They should be very clear about their privacy statements, terms, and condition policies.

Some of the features of a proper trading system can be the following. Is the trading be done automatically? There should be proper charts available to you based on historical and current fundamental and technical analysis. Current news and an updated database should be an integral part of your system. Ensure that you can contact the people behind the system if any difficulties arise. Most importantly, cushions should be provided to cover your risks.

When you use trading robots or software, you don't have to market yourself and hence don't have to be involved every minute of the day. The chances of any error that can be conducted by humans are dropped to almost zero. The possibility of missing the trades due to your unavailability is reduced. You don't have to wait for sideways or non-trending markets.

There are many options and application in a forex platform. The forex platform can display real-time executable quotes, real time charts, streaming news, live market commentary, one click dealing, trailing stop orders, remote access, upgrades, and much more. It is an excellent way to keep all of your forex trading information is one spot. It can also track your history and find what moves were successful and which ones were unsuccessful.

Chapter 4: The Keys To Successful Forex Trading Online

This information is created for anyone who has an interest in forex trading online to generate income part-time or full-time. New traders will need to learn the basic principles of the foreign exchange market before starting While experienced traders can consider this a refresher in forex trading online.

There are four steps to follow if you are considering trading forex online. However, their order is not particularly important; the most crucial part is their content to which the great attention and responsibility should be paid.

Forex Trading Online - The First Step

Choosing the right Forex Trading Agent online is your first step. You could have a great strategy, good technical analysis skills or an outstanding intuition but you will ultimately fail if you choose a bad trader.

A good forex agent is one that will not rip-off your money but will perform real trading with your positions and will back up your preferred deposit, withdraw methods, and has fast and helpful user support service. Look for a broker that is registered with some governmental financial ombudsman.

Probably the most important aspects of the agent are it's trading platform - but for a new trader, this part is not so crucial as for expert traders. Still, you'll want to trade with some powerful and informative platform as a MetaTrader or its analogs. For new traders, the more imperative is a demo account, which is often used to trade virtual money while you are training your forex skills. If you're a new trader, start only with the demo account!

Don't lose your cash on your first mistakes! Take advantage of learning forex trading using a demo account even if you are eager to start earning money -play it cautious!

Forex Trading Online - The second step

Learning fundamentals of forex trading is an important second step. If you have already found your Forex Trading Online broker, you will easily get all information from its website or user support. There are numerous articles and websites dedicated to forex basics in the World Wide Web. All you have to do is just Google for "forex trading basics" and you'll find everything you wanted plus much more. This approach shouldn't be underestimated, because aiming to trade without learning the market works is not only very risky, it will also become boring soon.

Forex Trading Online - Third step

Education is a crucial third step to forex trading online. FX Trading Education is not similar to any other training you probably have got in your life. Forex Trading market is very chaotic, so is the training - there are no fixed rules and all-time laws, it is unstable and dynamical. Therefore, to be on the top, you must learn new things about Forex Trading regularly and constantly. Aim to read plenty of books, articles other traders' opinions as you can. The more you learn, the more educated you will be. Also, with good Foreign exchange education, you will be able to create very sophisticated and efficient trading strategies.

Forex Trading Online - Fourth step

To achieve the successful results in Forex Trading market, you need to develop your very own strategies. While you are learning, you'll be satisfied with known strategies and probably even forex signals. However, true goal, which results in successful forex trading, is always to develop your strategies. Not one strategy, but to follow the market day by day, developing new strategies and improving those who began to fail. Also, this comes not only to the trading strategy (this part is obvious) but also to the money management strategy (this part is often underestimated). While you gain experience of trading, you'll inevitably build such strategies that will fit your trading style, you character, and your life as best as they can. Also, after that, trading can become a genuine pleasure, which will eventually result in your financial freedom.

If you're considering forex trading online, and you don't know where to get started, then you're in the right place. By reading this article, you will know all there is to know about forex trading, as well as where to go to find the best tips and trick from real professionals. Just don't rely on this to pay your bills or anything of the sort, at first.

At the beginning of your forex trading online career, you should keep several things in mind! As previously mentioned, you shouldn't rely on this to pay the bills, at least until you know how everything functions. Also, be sure to remember not to trade money you can't afford losing. It's certain that you're going to make mistakes when you're just starting out, and it's almost certain that you're going to lose your starting capital.

Even though it may seem complicated, creating a forex trading account is very easy, and is required on all sites that allow trading. You'll just have to insert some personal details, and you'll be ready to use your account and start trading! You should, however, take some time to study all the material provided on most sites, as this will allow you to get a better understanding of how exactly the trading system works!

You should learn everything there is to learn about currency trading too because it's key to becoming a successful online trader. You'll see that it's not very complicated, but it does require your complete attention. You will lose money if you're away from your PC when certain important events happen, and the prices rise or drop abruptly.

Out of a vast number of forex trading robots out there, there isn't even one that can get you acceptable results! Even though they may seem fair at first, and make you some money, after a while, they will start losing, and they'll probably lose your initial investment. Forex trading requires your complete attention, and you can't let a robot handle your money!

As mentioned before, creating a forex trading account isn't complicated, but after you create it, you'll have to decide if you want a demo account or a live account. Demo accounts use fake money, and they're used at first until you get used to the system. Why lose your hard-earned money when you can use a demo account and not lose any money? However, you also don't make any money, no matter how well you do, better keep that in mind! Just open a live account and deposit some money, so you can start making money!

There are numerous sites available that claim to show you how to become a successful forex trader, however not many hire real professionals for this purpose. Many don't even tell you about currency trading! If you want to be one of the best traders, you have to be trained by the best there are! Why trade forex if you don't make money from it, right?

If searching for one of the best places to get your forex trading online career on a roll, then you have to check out Harry's site. It offers all the information you need to start your trading on the right foot, and you can either open accounts, demo or live, to see how it goes.

Chapter 5: Forex Technical Analysis

Should you be a new foreign exchange (currency trading) speculator, currency trading technical analysis may seem like brain surgery. You may well also mistake it for fundamental research. Even though the two can need analysis, obviously, they're on the complete opposite end of each other regarding the subjective-objective spectrum. Understanding how fx functions and how both kinds of evaluation can be completed will enable you better to reach your goals in trading overseas foreign currencies.

What is fx?:

As with any investment decision, you've got to be aware what investment or security you are handling. In this as with any investment decision, you've got to know what asset or security you are working with. In this situation, you might be dealing with international currencies that you'll be able to buy or sell for making a profit primarily based on their changing values. The truth is that buying and selling foreign currencies could be incredibly risky. This can be because they can change their prices significantly inside a quick period. Nevertheless, if you are smart enough to evaluate the movements, you can make a massive income from this.

Basic evaluation in international currencies:

Due to the fact, the danger is excellent when coping with overseas trade, it is essential to get some prediction method. In which situation, unique kinds of examination can help you forecast how a forex will react.

Fundamental analysis, for instance, tends to make use of national politics, economic climate, and unexpected events, and then combines these factors collectively to create up the general situation. The investor looks in the general circumstance and makes a prediction concerning how that scenario will affect the foreign currency. For instance, if a country loses their leader, the actual foreign currency of their country might all of a sudden decline in worth.

Technical analysis in foreign currencies:

The currency trading technical analysis does not take care of circumstances, however with natural, unemotional Information. Rather than reading through the news, the particular trader takes a glimpse into the recent past of the currency's prices. This dealer may perhaps examine months' of currency value if she or he desires to see the bigger picture. After that, he or she may plot charts primarily based on the information to generate the progression or perhaps trending less difficult to read. Because of the employment of indicators, for instance, moving averages as well as Bollinger bands, the dealer will discover a structure or trend. She or he may additionally recognize whenever a currency exchange is going through a deadlock. A deadlock or being in a condition of congestion implies that the currency exchange is locked within a small range of prices. This may suggest that the currency is low-risk or not a lot can be gained through trading that value.

The benefits of currency trading technical analysis:

For some pros, forex trading analysis may be self-sufficient when generating predictions and pursuing trends. Because of forex trading analysis, you do not need to grow to be an economist or even a political analyst; you only have to be a fx trader who can plot as well as study graphs. Via the graphs, you'll be able to figure already out what is likely to occur the next day or even the subsequent week. Nonetheless, you ought to function with the knowledge that even forex trading technical analysis may be fallible. However, at the very least, it could give you a far better a foothold when coping with a high-risk security, for example, foreign money, which can be much better when compared with fumbling for your future investing decision.

Chapter 6: Forex Charts

It is common for inexperienced traders to think that forex trading is tough. The good news is, making money by trading foreign currencies is certainly not impossible as long as you are willing to educate yourself on the necessary skills. Similar to other moneymaking models, currency trading also incorporates many elements.

For instance, this kind of income generator has many types of tools that you can employ. One of the most well known is termed forex chart. A chart will enable you to evaluate what is happening to various currency pairs in real time. Such a tool is paramount to carry out technical analysis on forex market data.

Utilizing a chart, a trader can figure out how the market behaves. Experienced traders fully understand different patterns like Symmetrical Triangles, Double Top and Head and Shoulders that often show up on charts. By considering the models, it is possible for them to predict the right moments to place an order.

Reading a forex chart is not that difficult. It displays the activities of a particular currency pair within a specified period. When you observe a daily chart, recognize that a candle represents the price action of a single day. A candle at the same time presents some other vital facts such as the highest and lowest price on a certain day.

These days, you can find many charting programs available on the internet. Besides featuring the price actions, they often also come preloaded with some additional features such as programmable alerts and built-in strategies. If you plan to get one, make sure that it supports your ideas.

Forex charts are a vital tool for traders. With the aid of them, you can predict the future activities of various foreign currencies. It will be much less difficult for you to make smart decisions using a sophisticated charting software. Just remember also to grab the necessary skills to ensure that such tools will not be a total waste of your time and money.

If you're serious about currency buying and selling, you then ought to find out about forex trading graphs. You also have to know the way to interpret them. If you can master this particular art, then you're positive to create some major moolah here. Several experts say that trading successfully could be impossible any time you do not know the basics.

The actual role of these forex charts is to help you know the value of the currency at a particular point in time. The variation in the values is depicted in the form of graphs, and you can study them. Some of these charts are quite easy to study as well as interpret, and they have become an excellent source of information to many traders nowadays. If you want to take your trading to the next level, you need to know the importance of these charts.

It is necessary to observe the currency graphs carefully due to the fact it's especially tough to come across the proper opportunity to generate moolah when the values change. You will need to acquire that out by evaluating the data that you simply get via these graphs. Not only individuals but also numerous providers use these graphs as the source for details. It is a very nice option to study the existing marketplace trends.

You can find particularly a lot of websites which offer you access to these graphs if you are genuinely keen on them. If you can essentially do a bit of study on the net by spending some time, you will entirely fully grasp everything about currency trading charts and learn how to interpret them. Apart from these net web sites, you may also obtain them along with your buying software package if you are making use of any. It can be crucial to have access to them on an everyday basis to figure out the scenario. These days there, some excellent computer software programs, which allow you to take the proper decision and you, need to know about them.

At the end of the day, you cannot make it big here if you don't know how to interpret the charts. These charts can give you an idea of the past trends as well as the present ones so that you will gain a better picture of what will happen in the next few minutes. This will surely guide you to take a better decision. Only a few people can do the job of interpreting the data in the most accurate way. If you want to focus on this area, you need to master that skill.

It is quite important to know about several things that are related to the trading practices if you want to see yourself making some real money in the area of trading. Therefore, apart from getting some good software if you can learn and understand the basics of interpreting the forex charts, then you can surely see yourself taking money making decisions. So it's time you research more to know better about the charts that change the fortune of many people.

Chapter 7: Forex Price Action Trading

Are you quite interested in Forex trading or price action trading? Would you like to learn more? In these two distinct fields, do you wish to be proficient? If so, you have arrived at the best place. Everything you should learn about price action or about how precisely to learn Forex, one can learn from a course online. All you will need to do is make sure you know which course will be the most beneficial concerning learning price action or learning Forex trading. Surely, you need to think about this.

Finding the various online course that offers different price action trading, or Forex trading information and facts for you to learn is the first thing that you can do. You ought to compare the different courses and see which ones are likely to teach you the most beneficial information as the majority of these courses must have an overview of the different things that you will be learning on their site. You need to make certain that, regarding Forex trading, for example, the course will teach you what Forex trading exactly is, the various ways you can participate in Forex trading, the best time to trade Forex, etc.

You might want to seek out people who are in price action or Forex trading and see if they have experience with any of these courses. When it comes to finding people that are interested in these topics, a great way to do that is to utilize social networking or to go on numerous discussion boards and online forums. Without a doubt, you will find that you can find people who are thinking about the same things that you are interested in, and these individuals will be able to supply you with advice on how to go forward.

If you search for others who are more experienced with Forex trading or perhaps price action trading, they also may have strategies of courses that you can take that you did not uncover on your own. They may direct you along the same path that they took whenever they were learning Forex trading or price action trading, and you may find that is the most appropriate thing because they're experienced in this area. Additionally, you might get suggestions on particular courses to avoid.

The thing is, you will be able to discover more than enough information on the internet to help you learn Forex trading or price action trading if you do your research and look around and examine all of your options, and that will undoubtedly be a great thing in the long run. You can learn any new set of skills if you put in the correct amount of effort and time.

One thing essential to Forex trading success is having confidence in the system you are trading. Confidence is what allows you to place the business with the expectation of a positive result, even after suffering losses. Using price action setups is a great way to build the confidence you need to succeed finally as a Forex trader.

What one of the most common mistakes inexperienced traders make in the beginning is overcomplicating their trading system? They think if they add a ton of indicators to their charts it will cut out the losing trades. They believe that there must be some magical mix that only produces winning trade after winning trade. Ironically, this approach leads to lack of confidence in the system. They get so much information, a lot of times conflicting information, that they never feel comfortable with the decision to enter the market. Then when that inevitable losing trade comes, they become even more frustrated and less confident.

The best thing about price action trade setups is they are easy to identify. When a price action setup is identified, it is easy to know what to do, especially if you have a trading plan. Keeping things simple like this builds the confidence that you have an "edge" over the market. With that trust, you can place the trades with a positive expectation.

The hardest thing new traders need to realize is no trading system is perfect. Trying to make it perfect by overcomplicating your trading is only going to lead to a loss of confidence in your system every time there is an inevitable loss. Therefore, the first thing you need to do is accept that every system is going to suffer losses from time to time. However, gaining the confidence of using price action setups keeps you trading simple and allows you to identify trading opportunities and get into the market with an edge. This edge is going to lead to more winning trades than losers and a growing trading account.

I think the real problem is the lack of experience traders have before they abandon a trading system. Let us say you get a price action setup and it loses the first trade. Does this mean you should stop looking for that particular setup? Not, but that is what many traders do? Therefore, the only way to gain confidence in your price action trading system is to acquire valuable experience by trading it over time.

Chapter 8: Forex Indicators

It is not easy trying to come up with a successful forex trading system. In fact, some people never manage to do so and end up losing lots of money. Other people find success through buying a commercial trading system or learning how to trade from a mentor or professional trader. So what are the characteristics of a profitable forex trading system?

Well, everyone's system is different and unique in its way, but many of the most profitable trading systems share the same qualities. The first of these qualities is repetition. The best systems find the same types of high probability set-ups and trade them repeatedly.

This is the reason why so many forex traders to make trading decisions use technical analysis. Technical analysis is a way of displaying various trading patterns, so by finding a combination of technical indicators that are good at predicting future price moves, you can use these symbols to show these reoccurring and potentially profitable trading patterns.

Forex trading should be like a full-time job where you trade the same system every single day. Every trade should be like the preceding one, and there should be a tiny difference between one business and the next. You need to develop a system that can detect future price moves with a reasonable success rate and then only stick to this system all the time.

Another characteristic of a profitable trading system is that they will nearly always use solid money management rules. Therefore, they will only risk a small percentage of their bank on any one trade. A good system also generally applies strict stop loss standards and will target price moves that are further away than this stop loss level. This means that you can still make money from a particular trading system even if you have a modest win/loss ratio because of your winning trades more than make up for your losing ones.

Some of the most profitable systems go one step further and will use a strict stop loss, but instead of having a fixed target price for exiting a trade, they will let their winning trades run for as long as possible with the use of a trailing stop. This is another way that people make money from forex trading without necessarily having a very high win/loss ratio.

So overall, a profitable forex trading system will use a tight stop loss policy and will have a greater profit objective or will let their winning trades run. They also trade the same trading patterns repeatedly and do not deviate from this strategy.

Chapter 9: Forex Demo Accounts

Forex trading can be your road to making big bucks but the beginning of this road may not be smooth, and it may take you a while to get used to driving your trading accounts and learning to maneuver the corners and pitfalls of the forex market. Forex education process can be an equally expensive if you blindly jump into the market without preparation.

Forex brokers offer you the options of high leverages, which can lead to making bad sized risky trades, which may ruin your account terribly. The good news is that one can learn forex in a non-detrimental way by using a tool popularly known as Demo Trading Account.

A forex demo account is a feature offered by most brokers. It is a demo account which comes with a fictional account balance. It behaves the same way a real account behaves regarding market movements, trades, and leverages. You can practice and learn about trading using these accounts without the risk of losing out on real money as the money is just virtually there in your account. Let's see how practicing on a demo account, whether you are starting out or you are an experienced forex player, is always a good idea.

Free and easily available:

Brokers free of cost provides demo accounts. All they need is your name and email address. They offer you these trial versions for different durations; a good broker will offer you a demo account for unlimited time. It is always optional for you to register a real account with the same broker so you can try other as many agents before you decide on one.

Test a trading system or a software tool:

Developing a trading system is one of the most important things for forex success. Forex demo accounts offer you to test your trading ideas, strategies and software tools (indicators or robots) without risking your money.

Helps you understand the trading platform:

The forex broker provides you with a trading platform but understanding it and learning to use it comfortably can take time. A demo account will help you test all functions and explore all options of the without the risk of losing anything and in case you are not happy with it, you can always change to a broker with a better platform.

Helps you learn risk management:

Risk management is the key to real trading. Demo accounts effectively teach you to manage your risks in the market. They help you make your mind about trade sizes and risk sizes, which you want to use for your system with no real money on the line.

Demo accounts can prove effective training grounds, giving you the forex education, the trade practice that you need to become good at forex without learning things the hard way.

Chapter 10: Forex Robots

Forex robots are great tools to use when trading Forex because the market moves extremely fast. However, how do they do it? How do they track your currency pairs, help you use your strategies, and help you make gains?

The truth is that these are carefully programmed robots that are designed to function in a variety of ways. For instance, Forex robots are designed to identify trends. These trends are based on some factors and can be tough to calculate manually. This gives the robot the ability to have an idea of what may happen next.

Preventing losses:

When avoiding losses, you have control over how Forex robots behave. You can set limits. If a currency falls below a certain point, then you can tell the program not to let you lose any more money than that. This is how you can keep from wiping out your bank account. Wiping out your bank account can be a dangerous thing, which is something that you don't want to watch it happen at all. However, even Forex robots cannot keep you from losing some money because the forex market is unpredictable but more stable than other markets.

However, don't think that Forex robots are invincible because they are not. Remember that you make all the calls.

Achieving Gains:

Achieving gains are the goals of Forex robots. It is true that you are going to be able to gain more with a Forex robot instead of just doing it on your own. Yes, there are those professional investors making millions and not using any software. However, it can be rather difficult to do all of the reading to learn everything that you need to know about Forex to make it big.

Forex robots are perfect for beginners, but it is still important to educate yourself on Forex. Those with an education on the subject achieve more than those who only jump in. As with anything, you don't want just to jump in, and Forex robots are certainly no exception. This is because you will be putting some of your money on the line.

Nevertheless, you can see an average of a 75% return and see returns of up to 300% as your experience grows. The goal is to make Forex trading your income, but even as extra income it can give you a financial success. You can go to work, and your Forex robots can take care of your trades.

If you are unfamiliar with what Forex is, then the chances are that you are not going to know what

Forex Robots are, let alone how they perform their job. To allow you to understand fully how Forex Robots work, it is important that you know that Forex is the market of trading currencies of all different types. However, the Forex Market provides a futuristic form of exchanging currency. This is possible through the Forex Robot.

In addition, this is how you see success in Forex.

Chapter 11: Forex Reviews

There are a good number of traders who rely on gut instinct to make their trading decisions. Very rarely are the results successful as these decisions are based merely on luck. This is the reason why nearly 95% of all people who trade in the foreign exchange market incur such heavy losses. If you are are thinking of getting into forex trading, you have to rely instead on a solid forex education and a sound forex trading system instead of plucking your choices out of thin air.

Over the years, many traders have sought reliable trading systems to help them on their way to forex success. There are a lot of forex trading systems offered up for sale online, and some of these are so highly commercialized and promise immeasurable success that they appear too good to be true. To make a quick buck off gullible novice traders, some fraudulent individuals pass themselves off as seasoned brokers claiming to know the secrets to becoming forex millionaires. They offer their so-called tested and proven trading system for sale, and those who are unwary enough fall for it completely.

First, before going on a search for the best forex trading system, you will need to learn all the basics about the foreign exchange market. Find out how it works and what you need to do. Once you have a solid forex background, you can start searching for a system that will work for you.

Most forex trading systems have been designed to do many things, and you will need to determine what you need before settling on any one system. Some systems are geared at detecting market signals, some alert you to what may turn out to be profitable opportunities, and some prompt you to trade based on a currency curve, while others simply react to every change in the market. Find out which system is suited for you, whether you are a beginner or an expert trader.

To avoid being scammed, or trying system after frustrating system to find one that works for you, you will first need to do your research. While you can search the Internet for reliable forex trading systems, it will take a lot of time, patience, and determination on your part as there are hundreds, if not thousands of them in existence. Some of the most useful information about reliable trading systems can be found in third-party forex reviews. Make sure that the forex reviews you read online are objective, and not paid advertisements or testimonials posted by companies selling forex trading systems.

Another method of finding the best forex trading system is to join forex trading forums where you will find like-minded traders who have had experience with a good number of systems.

Interacting with all these fellow forex traders is even better than reading forex reviews as you are getting first-hand experiences from people who have been there.

Further check forex reviews if the trading system of your choice operates on a reliable web-based platform, as well as possesses 24-hour email or phone support should you have any issues that need attending to.

With an enough forex trading expertise and a sound system, success in forex trading is a good possibility.

Chapter 12: Forex Day Trading

Day Trading is the purchasing and marketing of financial instruments within the same trading day where the trader squares off or liquidate all positions by the end of the trading day. In foreign currency trading, a day refers to the trading hours in any of the four market sessions (Sydney, Tokyo, London or New York).

In contrast to position traders who would wait out the 24-hour forex market until price objectives are reached, forex day traders confine their trading activities within the trading hours of the particular session they are in. They don't "wait out the market" instead; they take advantage of small price movements and are contented with making small but consistent profits. A day trader is akin to a 'scalper' (or one who scalps for profit) and employs an almost similar strategy of getting in and out of the market fast. Contrary to popular opinion, day trading can be profitable as long as one prepares himself adequately before engaging in the trade.

There are a lot of successful and well-known day traders around. Many of whom have built fortunes out of day trading. Most of them employ their forex day trading systems which unfortunately most of them are also not too willing to share with others!

This leads us to ask 'what makes up an effective day trading system?'

An efficient day trading system is:

One which can identify and take advantage of every market opportunity that presents itself.

One which is equipped with trading tools that include charting software that can assist in determining short-term price trends, establish where minor and major resistances and supports are, takes stock of pending price reversals before they even happen.

One which can calculate exact entry and exit points, generate a buy and sell signals for you.

One which has a built in stop loss mechanism in place.

One which employs an efficient money management strategy.

One which generates more profitable trades than losses.

One that sets a profit objective for you for the day and stops you from trading when the target has been reached.

One which can prove its profitability with back testing.

Many automated forex day trading systems are being sold on the market today. All of them claim to have generated substantial profits. All of them are claiming to be the best. However, what is good for others may not be good for you. Therefore, if and when you do decide to get one of them, make sure it has all the requisites of an efficient day trading system as enumerated above. It can be back tested and should be able to produce favorable results on back testing. Most important of all, it should come with a 30-day money back guarantee to ensure that you can get your money back.

You should know something else. Two-thirds of upstart forex day traders lose their shirts. The other third lose their pants! Wizen up and refuse to be part of this statistic. Get the adequate knowledge and develop the necessary skills to be a day trader before you even try to make that first trade.

Chapter 13: Managed Forex Accounts

The foreign exchange or the forex marketplace as it is a lot more fondly known as is one of the great opportunities for investment that prevail in the market today. Plenty of investors are looking methods to diversify into the foreign exchange marketplace and benefit the liquidity being offered in the global foreign exchange market. Although you will discover stocks, debt marketplace, and mutual funds, investing in the forex market is still one of the most sought-after alternatives simply because nothing comes close to it when talking about the potentials for trading within the Forex marketplace. Investing in the forex market via managed forex accounts will reap much better and much more benefits for you. There's a vast market for additional speculative trading within the exchange of two various currencies.

Acquiring Began with Forex Trading:

Just before you set your foot within the trading world, you'll find specific things that you'll want to do and which is opening a trading account. It is the most important aspect before you could begin within the shuffling world of trading. It typically depends on the broker or finance manager whom you chose to open managed forex accounts with, but it starts with a deposit of $200 and up. Then you're now ready to kick off. All of the transactions of your forex managed funds will be in your name and not of the broker or your finance manager or that of the management business. All that they do is study the market carefully, figure out the trend and make the necessary recommendations to you. The final decision on where to invest is still yours, and they'll have no access to withdraw from your forex managed funds.

Investing inside the Forex Marketplace:

The forex marketplace is not purely just about investment and trading opportunities. Just like in any other organization, you'll want to have strategies, investment strategies which are, and you'll want to have a wide span of knowledge regarding the forex marketplace, foreign currencies, and their fluctuation rates. You also require knowing about geopolitics, strong and weak pairs of currencies, and also the distinction between the base currency and its counter currency. As a lot as you would like to be successful with your investment in managed forex accounts, you have to be technically aware of all of the issues in the forex marketplace, investing, and in trading.

Why Choose Managed Forex Accounts:

One of the reasons why men and women decide on to invest in managed forex accounts is due to the fact somebody else takes care of all their forex investing requirements. Professionals who have long been inside the trading company complete these. Who else would know any far better about the trading business and market performance than them?

Other reasons for opting managed forex accounts are:

- Asset Diversification

- Liquidity of Investments

- Real Time Account Management

- Liquidity of Assets

Invest Now:

For initial time retail investors or even those who have been in the trading enterprise for a long time and yet do not have the time to watch their investments closely, then you need the services of the specialists. They might answer all your queries about the foreign exchange market plus the complex trading business. Forex brokers are out there to assist you together with your investments and guarantee that there is no way that you'll curse your managed forex accounts.

Chapter 14: Forex Trading Basics

Forex market involves the trading of currencies from different countries and traders need to learn Forex trading basics for their businesses to be successful, and they should also find out how to implement them.

A Forex trader should always choose a currency pair that is bound to change in its value within a short period, and identify the best market place where he or she can effectively trade.

The business can be carried out trough a broker or a market maker so that the middleman can pass the order to the relevant partner in the interbank market who will fill your position. When a person is satisfied with the level of trade that he has engaged in, he can choose to close the deal; the middleman will also close his position immediately in the interbank market. Forex trading basics will help you to engage in successful business and make reasonable profits.

There are many Forex trading basics, and one of them is the Forex orders. Different types of rules in the Forex market helps businesspersons to control their trades. They control how you enter and how you exit a Forex trade. Market orders are used to open or close a trade at the prevailing market price.

On the other hand, limit orders are used to exit the market in profits. A limit order is often the goal of many traders because significant gains are realized to their account balances. Stop orders are exits that will close down a dealers business. It closes the trade at a designated level of a loss and can be used to lock in gains at a time when the business is making profits. Entry orders are used at the time of entering the stock market. Understanding the rules as a part of Forex trading basics, helps you to employ risk management practices and is an essential and fundamental skill for a blooming business.

Forex charts are a vital part of Forex because it is considered as a unique science of the trade. Learn how to read the charts because they always seem complicated at first, but with regular lessons, it becomes easier to master the way the charts flow.

The charts are also different depending on the options that a trader uses. For beginners, it is advisable to start learning with easy options as you progress to complex chart options. Each chart also has different settings, which display the style of the prevailing market price and the type of period that a trader needs to view at a particular time. The period varies from 1 second to 10 years because of the different chart systems. For a smooth Forex trading, traders and brokers should learn how to read Forex quotes with ease, as they are vital Forex trading basics for a sound business.

The other technical and essential skill are moving averages. This technical indicator helps traders to keep track of the pricing trend of different currencies. "Stop loss" are also important Forex trading basics and dealers should learn how to use them.

Chapter 15: Risk Control

Currency dealing is not an easy business and requires much effort on the part of investors. Often, people it difficult to get along with the reasons for this market that even easy guidelines are unpleasant. Inappropriate Forex Risk Management Solution are usually the reason why disadvantages and problems come your way. Having an efficient dealing plan and method is sometimes not enough in attaining your goals and neither can a variety of resources raise your transaction account. One of the typical issues of investors is that they have been keeping on duplicating what errors they have done from their previous dealing encounter. However, of course, you could never obtain achievements in dealing if you let your feelings intrude your company. Luckily, issues like this could be quickly fixed with just a spread of self-discipline and right mindset towards the accomplishment of objectives.

However, most investors seemed to be not acquainted with the threats they are taking. Also, because of that, they don't succeed to perform appropriate currency trading risk control to be able to fix the coming up issue. Risk Management Solution is effective only if you know how much you are willing to treat while supposing for how much earnings you will obtain at the end. Failures and disadvantages are just a cause of too much status on the dropping place. Many investors aren't conscious that the more time they will keep on their dropping business, the greater their threats are and the likelihood of obtaining future economic problems or more intense, bankruptcy.

To better help you with currency dealing threat control, you also need to know how to determine the risk-reward rate. This way, you have a concept of the variations between how much you are going to generate as well as the aspect of your financial commitment you are going to reduce. With this understanding, you are well knowledgeable of the potential results of your company as well as help you in developing your activity programs. Moreover, establishing for a stop-loss is also valuable. Not only it identifies restrict of your approved reduction, but it also stops further harm to your other sources and financial commitment strategies. There are still a lot of methods on how to better enhance your earnings and change the threats you are getting. You just have to be accountable enough to look for other indicates of attaining your objectives. Intellect alone is not enough to be able to obtain achievements, but being sensible to deal with each challenging scenario and having a successful technique could be the key to having a well-rewarded dealing result.

If organizations are looking for exposure to handling cash, assets, financial threat, protect bookkeeping and conformity all through a single remedy; they are looking for features that define a Treasury and Risk Control (TRM) remedy. These days, when industries modify is instant and regulating modifies reacts in kind, smooth information, and fast time-to-market is critical. Software-as-a-Service (SaaS) can provide. A TRM remedy that controls the reasoning abilities exposure within a company so that they can function and contend in the new world.

Chapter 16: Trading Discipline

What makes an F1 racing champion? Is it the car? Is it the technology that went into building the engines? No, it is the driver. The driver's confidence around corners and patience in the face of a daunting challenge by other drivers makes a champion. Similarly, the trader makes the difference in stock and options trading. It is the stock or options traders' confidence in their chosen methodology and their patience in the face of daunting price changes that makes a champion stock or options trader.

Trading Confidence and Trading Discipline are the most important aspects of trading psychology that make millionaire stock or options brokers. They are also the main motive why so many stocks and options traders fail and break their bank.

Trading Psychology - Trading Assurance

Trading trust is a mental confidence banking account in every trader, and trading discipline determines if you deposit or withdraw from it. Trading confidence is what enables every stock and options traders to execute trades according to their chosen methodology confidently and to stick to the game despite losses knowing that they will eventually make more wins than losses. Trading confidence is a banking account, which you can either deposit to or withdraw from. Each time you lose money, you pull out from your trading confidence and each time you make money, you deposit to your trading confidence. When your trading trust is zero or bankrupt, you will find yourself hesitating before every trade while imagining the pain if the trade turns out a loser again. You will have sleepless nights and will rush out of trades at the very first sign of danger, making unnecessary losses. When that happens, it is the time to go back to paper and re-examine the way you have been trading. In fact, you do not have to break your trading account balance to have your trading confidence bankrupt and a bankrupt trading trust always lead to a bankrupt trading account. Conversely, every time you win money with your chosen methodology, you deposit to your trading confidence bank, feel confident and joyful when placing trades and do not panic when trades go wrong.

Trading Psychology - Factors Affecting Trading Confidence:

A major determinant of your level of trading confidence is the amount and nature of money that you have to trade with. The more money you can afford to lose, the higher your initial level of trading confidence. Stock and options traders whom can afford to lose only very little money would usually have very low level of trading confidence as every loss takes a significant bite out of their trading confidence bank. Again, you need not lose all your money to lose all your trading confidence. Some stock and options traders no longer feel confident enough to trade when their account go down by 30%, while some reach that level of confidence bankrupt only when their account go down by 70%. The nature of money you have to trade with also determines your starting trading confidence. If you were trading with excess money, which you do not need, then your level of trading confidence would be very high. In fact, your trading confidence could still be high even if you lose all that money. Conversely, if you were trading with borrowed money, which you need to pay back in installment, and with interest, your trading confidence would be extremely low as every loss makes it harder for you to pay the money back.

Alas, there is no objective and empirical method of calculating your level of trading confidence and most stock and options traders only understand it when it goes bankrupt.

At this point, it is clear that you need to win money to build up a strong trading confidence banking account and to win money; you need to follow a proven and successful trading methodology. A losing method will bankrupt your trading trust in no time no matter how much you start out with.

Trading Psychology - Trading Discipline:

Once you are sure that you have a proven and successful method like my Star Trading System, you will need Trading Discipline to make sure you stick to the rules and trade only when entry requirements are fully met. Without trading discipline, you will end up spoiling any successful methodology, leading to a withdrawal of your trading confidence.

Trading Discipline consists of Patience and a Calm, Objective mind.

Every trading methodology trades only when specific setups or rules are met. Without trading discipline, you will not have the patience to wait for such setups or rules to be fully met before trading and every time you break the rules, you increase your odds of losing and every loss withdraws from your trading confidence. Therefore, do not make "fun" or "experimental" trades by compromising rules as losing under such conditions do withdraw from your trading confidence as well.

Trading Confidence & Complacence:

A distinction must be made here regarding trading confidence and complacency. Complacency comes not from a high trading confidence but a complete lack of trading discipline. Complacency always leads to a quick and complete bankrupt of trading confidence, so, be certain to understand the difference.

Trading Psychology:

Finally, the relationship between trading confidence and trading discipline goes both ways. A strong trading discipline following a proven methodology builds strong trading confidence and a strong trading confidence encourages the development of active trading discipline as you experience the success coming from following rules. Only when you have both strong trading confidence and trading discipline will you have the trading psychology needed to make millions.

Chapter 17: Forex Myths

If you have any experience of forex trading, you will probably have heard the three common beliefs mentioned in this article. However, it should be pointed out that, despite popular belief, they are complete myths and are false.

The first of these relates to learning how to trade forex. It's often pointed out by so-called experts that one of the best ways to learn how to trade is to place paper trades for a certain length of time. In other words, you write down the deals you would have theoretically made if you were trading a live account. To me, this is utterly pointless because anyone can do this, and it doesn't teach you anything about forex trading because nothing is at stake.

A much better option is to read as much as you can and learn from experienced forex traders before developing your forex trading system. Then start trading a live account but with very small stakes. This way there is emotion involved if you place a losing trade, even if it is only small stakes, so this motivates and pressurizes you into finely tuning your system so that the next trade is a winning one and the system becomes profitable overall.

The second misconception is that forex trading is easy. You will often see this statement made on sales pages when someone is trying to sell you their 'amazing' system. However, as an experienced trader myself, let me assure you that trading forex is anything but easy. Indeed this is borne out by the fact that only a tiny minority of people who try their hand at this potentially rewarding occupation make any money. It's a sad fact that most people will end up blowing their bankroll and quitting trading altogether, so it's certainly not easy.

The final misconception is that if you want to make the big money, then you have to be in front of your computer screen all day long to trade a lot of positions. This is false because if you switch to more extended periods, you can capture far bigger price moves which more than make up for all of these smaller trades. Also, it's a lot less stressful and far easier to make profits this way because technical analysis is so much more reliable on the longer time frames.

So if you ever hear someone come out with any of these statements, please ignore them because they are talking complete nonsense.

To Learn Forex:

As much as you give yourself time to learn the basics of the forex market, as well as some advanced ideas about it, it also helps to learn forex trading myths to keep yourself aware. These myths can as easily trick you into making the biggest mistakes in forex trading that can prove to be damaging, especially to newcomers to the currency market. More often than not, many foreigners fall into the array of forex traders who end up losing their money because they are all too caught up in believing that forex trading is a get-rich-quick scheme. This is just one of the many forex myths that you should learn so you can keep yourself from making the biggest forex trading markets that any trader can commit.

Forex trading is not a simple buy and sells the thing, and it does not offer any get-rich-quick promises. Currency trading requires a thorough understanding of what the different trading systems are and how you can use trading signals to your advantage. To learn forex trading basics is just the start. This unpredictable market might require you to go through a series of losses first before you can fully understand the different crafts used in the trade. Keep in mind that forex trading is far from a child's play.

With this said, it also helps to take note that forex trading is far from playing online casino games. There are those who equate trading to gambling, but this should not be the case. In forex trading, your success does not totally rely on luck. Your success can also be defined by how well you can understand and use macroeconomic indicators to your advantage.

If you think that forex trading is just for the rich and famous strategists, you can never be more wrong. The currency market is by far one of the easiest markets that newcomers can join. You simply need a computer, an internet connection, some spare time to spend on trading, and about a couple of dollars in capital. If you were able to spend enough time to learn forex basics and myths, you would be able to distinguish which things to do best in certain situations that will eventually help you rake in profits.

So remember, to learn forex basics is not enough. You should also learn about the different forex myths so you can develop ways son how to avoid them. Awareness can just become your key to success in this rewarding yet unpredictable market.

Conclusion

There is a definite step-by-step process to becoming a successful Forex trader. Most would-be traders don't become profitable on their first try, or even the second or third. However, those that take the journey and make it to consistent profits learn a lot along the way. Here are three things I feel are essential for becoming a Forex trading success story.

There are many different ways to trade Forex, from scalping the lower periods to trading on the daily and weekly sessions. Nevertheless, in my experience, the traders have the persistence and stamina to trade the higher periods that do the best. Lower periods are less reliable; ironically take more time in front of the computer and end up being more stressful than higher periods.

I was also drawn to the lower periods when I first started out. I thought I would be able to make more money and learn faster because setups happened faster and I could use reduced stop loss values. I wanted to pop into the market when it was convenient for me, make some quick cash and be done for the day. Nevertheless, the opposite happened. Hard to believe, but when I switched to higher periods, I started to enjoy more success. Therefore, the first tip for trading successfully is to trade on time frames no lower than 1 hour. (The period I trade on now is the 4-hour period).

New traders want to make more money on each trade by using big lot sizes. Many times this means using too tight of a stop loss instead of the proper stop loss based on price action. As a result, they are stopped out a lot and lower their winning percentage.

A better way to trade is to manage your risk with your lot size. Place your stop where the market tells you, and then adjust your lot size to manage risk. This way, you can determine a specific percentage of your account to risk on each trade, which will be the same regardless of whether your stop loss is 20 pips or 200 pips. Therefore, the next secret is to use your lot size to manage your risk.

Forex trading is a serious business, not a get-rich-quick scheme. From the first two recommendations, you can see that successful traders move away from the fast time frames and unrealistic stop losses are searching for quick profits. Treating Forex like gambling leads to losing, a lot of money and having your sporadic wins reward bad behavior that eventually destroys your trading account.

A better way is to have patience and treat your trading like a business. In the end, creating a trading plan for slow, steady profits and developing the trading skills to trading the plan consistently is what creates a successful trader. Forex trading should be treated as a serious business, because when you do, you can make serious money.

Please if you enjoyed this book and feel it gave you lots of value then I would greatly appreciate it if you gave an honest review of it. Those honest words would be more than just words to me but feedback for my next book!

Also, please check out my other books!

Thanks for reading my book.

CPSIA information can be obtained
at www.ICGtesting.com
Printed in the USA
LVOW13s0047180717

541653LV00028BA/652/P

9 781535 235693